Learn MS Dynamics CRM Customer Insights

The MS Dynamics CRM Customer Insights Module is a powerful tool that allows businesses to collect and analyze customer data. This data can be used to improve customer relationships, target marketing efforts, and increase sales. The module provides users with the ability to create custom reports and dashboards, as well as export data for further analysis. The MS Dynamics CRM Customer Insights Module is an essential tool for businesses that want to improve their customer relationships.

The book covers the following:

1. Introduction to MS Dynamics CRM Customer Insights Module:

Overview of customer insights and its importance in modern businesses

Introduction to MS Dynamics CRM Customer Insights Module and its key features

Benefits of using MS Dynamics CRM Customer Insights for data-driven decision-making

2. Getting Started with MS Dynamics CRM Customer Insights Module:

Installation and configuration of MS Dynamics CRM Customer Insights Module

Navigating the Customer Insights Module interface and key terminology

Setting up data sources and connections for customer data ingestion

3. Customer Data Integration and Data Management:

Integrating customer data from various sources (CRM, ERP, website, etc.)

Data cleaning, transformation, and enrichment for accurate insights

Managing and organizing customer profiles and attributes

4. Customer Segmentation and Audience Analysis:

Creating customer segments based on demographics, behaviors, and preferences

Analyzing customer segments for targeted marketing and personalization

Utilizing machine learning and predictive analytics for segmentation

5. Customer Journey Mapping and Analysis:

Mapping and analyzing customer journeys across touchpoints and channels

Understanding customer interactions, behaviors, and pain points

Optimizing customer journeys for enhanced engagement and conversions

6. Customer Lifetime Value and Churn Analysis:

Calculating customer lifetime value (CLV) and predicting churn

Identifying high-value customers and implementing retention strategies

Leveraging predictive analytics for CLV and churn analysis

7. Marketing Campaign Analysis and Optimization:

Analyzing marketing campaign performance and attribution

A/B testing and optimization of marketing campaigns

Utilizing customer insights for personalized and targeted marketing

8. Sales Forecasting and Opportunity Analysis:

Forecasting sales revenue and pipeline using customer insights

Analyzing sales opportunities and identifying upsell and cross-sell opportunities

Integrating customer insights with sales processes and workflows

9. Customer Service and Support Analytics:

Analyzing customer service interactions and satisfaction metrics

Implementing proactive support and personalized service strategies

Utilizing sentiment analysis and customer feedback for service improvements

10. Privacy and Data Governance:

Understanding data privacy regulations and compliance (e.g., GDPR, CCPA)

Implementing data governance and security measures

Ensuring ethical use of customer data and transparency in insights generation

11. Integration and Extensibility:

Integrating MS Dynamics CRM Customer Insights with other systems (e.g., CRM, marketing automation)

Extending the functionality through customizations, plugins, and workflows

Integration with external analytics and business intelligence tools

12. Best Practices and Advanced Tips:

Implementing industry best practices for customer insights management

Handling complex data scenarios and challenges

Optimizing performance and scalability of the Customer Insights Module

13. Future Trends and Developments:

Exploring the latest features and updates in MS Dynamics CRM Customer Insights Module

Understanding the roadmap and future direction of the Customer Insights Module

Predicting and discussing emerging trends in customer data analytics and insights

1. Introduction to MS Dynamics CRM Customer Insights Module:

The MS Dynamics CRM Customer Insights Module is a powerful tool that allows businesses to collect and analyze customer data. This data can be used to improve customer relationships, target marketing efforts, and increase sales. The module provides users with the ability to create custom reports and dashboards, as well as export data for further analysis. The MS Dynamics CRM Customer Insights Module is an essential tool for businesses that want to improve their customer relationships.

Overview of customer insights and its importance in modern businesses

In the modern business world, customer insights are more important than ever. With the advent of big data and the rise of data-driven decision making, businesses are increasingly relying on customer insights to guide their strategies.

Customer insights are the key to understanding what your customers want and need, and how they behave. By understanding your customers, you can develop targeted marketing campaigns, improve your products and services, and create a better overall customer experience.

There are many different ways to gather customer insights, but one of the most effective is through customer surveys. Surveys can help you understand what your customers think about your brand, their level of satisfaction with your products or services, and their overall buying habits.

Customer insights are also important for retention and loyalty. By understanding your customers, you can develop strategies to keep them coming back. And, by understanding their buying habits, you can develop loyalty programs that reward them for their business.

In today's competitive business environment, customer insights are essential for any company that wants to stay ahead of the curve. By understanding your customers, you can develop strategies to improve your products, services, and overall customer experience.

Introduction to MS Dynamics CRM Customer Insights Module and its key features

The MS Dynamics CRM Customer Insights Module is a powerful tool that provides users with valuable insights into their customers. The module allows users to view customer information in a variety of ways, including customer profiles, customer interactions, customer journeys, and customer touchpoints. The module also provides users with the ability to create and manage customer segments, as well as to create and manage customer journeys. Additionally, the module provides users with the ability to track customer engagement across channels, and to create and manage customer touchpoints.

Benefits of using MS Dynamics CRM Customer Insights for data-driven decision-making

The benefits of using MS Dynamics CRM Customer Insights for data-driven decision-making are many and varied. By having access to customer data, businesses can make more informed decisions about their marketing and sales strategies. Additionally, they can use this data to better understand their customers' needs and wants. This, in turn, can lead to improved customer satisfaction and loyalty.

2. Getting Started with MS Dynamics CRM Customer Insights Module:

Installation and configuration of MS Dynamics CRM Customer Insights Module

The MS Dynamics CRM Customer Insights Module is a powerful tool that can help organizations to understand their customers better and provide them with targeted and personalized service. The module can be installed and configured by following the instructions in the Getting Started with MS Dynamics CRM Customer Insights Module guide. After installation, the module can be accessed from the CRM main menu.

The module provides a number of features that can be used to understand customer behavior and preferences. These features include customer segmentation, customer profiling, customer journey mapping, and customer engagement scoring. The module also provides a number of reports and dashboards that can be used to track customer behavior and trends.

Organizations can use the MS Dynamics CRM Customer Insights Module to improve their

customer service and to better target their
marketing efforts. The module can also be used to
help identify opportunities for new products and
services.

Navigating the Customer Insights Module interface and key terminology

The Customer Insights Module interface can be a
bit daunting at first, but once you get the hang of it,
it's a powerful tool for understanding your
customers. Here are some key terms to help you
get started:

Data Model: The data model is the foundation of
the Customer Insights Module. It defines the
entities (e.g. customer, product, order, etc.) and
relationships (e.g. customer buys product) that are
used to build customer insights.

Dataset: A dataset is a collection of data that is
used to populate the entities in the data
model.Datasets can be imported from external
sources (e.g. CRM, ERP, marketing automation,
etc.), or they can be generated within the
Customer Insights Module itself.

Dimension: A dimension is an entity in the data model that represents a specific characteristic of a customer (e.g. gender, age, location, etc.).

Metric: A metric is a numerical value that represents a specific customer behavior (e.g. purchase amount, number of orders, number of returns, etc.).

Segment: A segment is a group of customers that share similar characteristics (e.g. all customers who live in the same city, all customers who bought the same product, etc.).

Now that you know some of the key terms, let's take a look at the interface.

The first thing you'll see when you open the Customer Insights Module is the Dashboard. The Dashboard is your home base, and it's where you can see an overview of all your customer data.

To the left of the Dashboard, you'll see the Navigation pane. This is where you can access all the different features of the Customer Insights Module.

The first section in the Navigation pane is the Data Model. This is where you can view and edit the entities and relationships in the data model.

The next section is Datasets. This is where you can import data from external sources, or generate datasets within the Customer Insights Module.

The next section is Dimensions. This is where you can view and edit the dimensions in the data model.

The next section is Metrics. This is where you can view and edit the metrics in the data model.

The next section is Segments. This is where you can view and edit the segments in the data model.

And finally, the last section is Insights. This is where you can see the insights that have been generated based on the data in the data model.

Now that you know the basics of the Customer Insights Module interface, you're ready to start exploring all the different features it has to offer.

Setting up data sources in MS Dynamics CRM Customer Insights and connections for customer data ingestion

It is important to set up data sources in MS Dynamics CRM Customer Insights in order to ensure customer data is ingested correctly. The first step is to create a connection for each data source. For example, if you are using Salesforce, you will need to create a Salesforce connection. To do this, go to the Connections page and click the "+" icon.

Next, select the type of connection you want to create. In this case, select Salesforce.

Enter the required information for the connection, such as the Salesforce URL, username, and password. Once the connection is created, you can then add the customer data sources.

To add a data source, go to the Data Sources page and click the "+" icon.

Select the type of data source you want to add. For example, if you want to add a Salesforce data source, select the Salesforce connection you created earlier.

Enter the required information for the data source, such as the name, description, and data source URL. Once the data source is added, you can then map the data fields.

To map the data fields, go to the Fields Mapping page and click the "+" icon.

Select the data source and data field you want to map. For example, if you want to map the

Salesforce data source field "Account Name" to the Customer Insights field "Name," you would select the Salesforce data source and the "Account Name" field.

Click the "Map" button to map the fields.

Repeat this process for each data source and data field you want to map. Once all the fields are mapped, you can then activate the data sources.

To activate a data source, go to the Data Sources page and click the "Activate" button.

Enter the required information for the activation, such as the start date and time, and then click the "Activate" button.

The data source is now activated and customer data will start flowing into MS Dynamics CRM Customer Insights.

3. Customer Data Integration and Data Management in MS Dynamics CRM Customer Insights

Integrating customer data from various sources (CRM, ERP, website, etc.)

As the world of business changes, so does the way that companies must manage their customer data. In the past, customer data was typically siloed in different departments and systems, making it difficult to get a complete view of the customer. Today, however, customer data integration (CDI) and data management in MS Dynamics CRM Customer Insights is critical for companies that want to stay ahead of the competition.

CDI allows companies to combine customer data from various sources (CRM, ERP, website, etc.) into a single, unified view. This complete view of the customer is then used to create targeted marketing campaigns, improve customer service, and make better business decisions.

Data management in MS Dynamics CRM Customer Insights is a critical part of CDI. It ensures that customer data is accurate, complete, and up-to-date. It also provides the necessary tools for cleansing and enriching customer data.

Overall, CDI and data management in MS Dynamics CRM Customer Insights are essential for companies that want to remain competitive in today's ever-changing business landscape.

Data cleaning, transformation, and enrichment for accurate insights in MS Dynamics CRM Customer Insights

Data is the lifeblood of any organization, and accurate data is essential for making sound decisions. For this reason, data cleansing, transformation, and enrichment are essential processes for ensuring that data is accurate and useful.

In Microsoft Dynamics CRM Customer Insights, data cleansing is used to remove errors and inconsistencies from data. This can be done manually or through automated tools. Data transformation is used to convert data from one format to another, such as from structured to unstructured data. Data enrichment is used to add additional information to data, such as demographics or customer profiles.

These processes are essential for ensuring that data is accurate and useful. Without them, data can be misleading or even useless. By cleansing, transforming, and enriching data, organizations can be confident that they are making decisions based on accurate and reliable information.

Managing and organizing customer profiles and attributes in MS Dynamics CRM Customer Insights

Organizing customer profiles and attributes in MS Dynamics CRM Customer Insights is a critical part of customer data integration and data management. By bringing all of your customer data into a central location, you can more easily see patterns and correlations that can help you better understand your customers. Additionally, by keeping your customer profiles and attributes organized, you can make it easier for other systems to access and use your customer data.

4 Customer Segmentation and Audience Analysis in MS Dynamics CRM Customer Insights

Creating customer segments in MS Dynamics CRM Customer Insights based on demographics, behaviors, and preferences

As the marketing manager for a small-to-medium sized business, you've been tasked with creating customer segments in MS Dynamics CRM Customer Insights. After doing some research, you've decided to base your segments on demographics, behaviors, and preferences.

To start, you gather all of the available data on your customers. This includes information like age, gender, location, purchase history, and any other relevant data points. Once you have this data, you begin to analyze it to look for patterns and trends.

For example, you might notice that most of your customers are women between the ages of 25 and 34. Based on this, you could create a customer segment for "young professional women." Or, you might notice that a lot of your customers live in a certain city and tend to purchase certain types of products. Based on this, you could create a customer segment for "urbanites who love to shop."

Once you've created your customer segments, you can start to create targeted marketing campaigns that are specifically designed to appeal to each segment. This helps to ensure that your marketing efforts are more effective and that your customers are more likely to convert.

Analyzing customer segments in MS Dynamics CRM Customer Insights for targeted marketing and personalization

As the marketing manager for a small to mid-size business, you are always looking for ways to improve your targeted marketing and personalization efforts. After hearing about MS Dynamics CRM Customer Insights, you decide to give it a try. After signing up for the service, you are quickly able to create customer segments based on a variety of factors, including purchase history, demographics, and even online behavior.

You are also able to track the performance of each segment, and see which segments are most responsive to your marketing campaigns. With this valuable information at your fingertips, you are able to fine-tune your marketing efforts and better target your audience, resulting in more sales and happier customers.

Utilizing machine learning and predictive analytics for segmentation in MS Dynamics CRM Customer Insights

Organizations are always looking for ways to better understand their customers and find new ways to target them with relevant messages and offers. One way to do this is through customer segmentation, which is the process of dividing customers into groups based on shared characteristics.

Machine learning and predictive analytics can be used to automatically segment customers in Microsoft Dynamics CRM Customer Insights. This is done by analyzing customer data and finding patterns that can be used to group customers together. The benefits of using machine learning for segmentation are that it is fast, accurate, and can be done at scale.

Organizations can use the segments generated by machine learning to create targeted marketing campaigns and offers. They can also use them to better understand their customers and what they are interested in. By using machine learning to segment customers, organizations can get a better return on investment from their marketing campaigns and improve the customer experience.

5. Customer Journey Mapping and Analysis in MS Dynamics CRM Customer Insights

Mapping and analyzing customer journeys across touchpoints and channels in MS Dynamics CRM Customer Insights

The process of mapping and analyzing customer journeys across touchpoints and channels in MS Dynamics CRM Customer Insights can be divided into two main steps:

1. Collecting data on customer journeys across touchpoints and channels

2. Analyzing this data to identify common patterns and areas for improvement

To collect data on customer journeys, MS Dynamics CRM Customer Insights uses a combination of surveys, interviews, and focus groups. This data is then analyzed to identify common patterns and areas for improvement.

Some of the common patterns that have been identified include:

- Customers often start their journey on one channel (such as online) and then move to another channel (such as in-store)
- Customers often have different journey paths depending on their needs (such as purchase vs. service)
- Customers often encounter difficulty when trying to contact a company through multiple channels

Based on these findings, MS Dynamics CRM Customer Insights recommends a few best practices for improving customer journeys:

- Make it easy for customers to move between channels
- Offer a consistent experience across all channels
- Make it easy for customers to contact a company through multiple channels

By following these best practices, companies can improve the overall customer experience and increase customer satisfaction.

Understanding customer interactions, behaviors, and pain points in MS Dynamics CRM Customer Insights

As a business analyst, understanding customer interactions, behaviors, and pain points is essential to creating an effective customer journey map. By analyzing data in MS Dynamics CRM Customer Insights, businesses can get a clear picture of where their customers are struggling and where they are succeeding. This information can then be used to create a customer journey map that highlights the key steps in the customer experience, as well as the pain points that need to be addressed. By understanding customer interactions and behaviors, businesses can make sure that their customer journey map is accurate and effective, leading to improved customer satisfaction and loyalty.

Optimizing customer journeys for enhanced engagement and conversions in MS Dynamics CRM Customer Insights

As the adoption of Microsoft Dynamics CRM Customer Insights continues to grow, so too does the need for organizations to optimize their customer journeys for enhanced engagement and conversions. Customer journey mapping and analysis is a powerful tool that can help organizations to identify areas of improvement and to make the necessary changes to improve the customer experience.

Organizations that have adopted Microsoft Dynamics CRM Customer Insights have seen a significant improvement in customer engagement and conversions. By using customer journey mapping and analysis, organizations are able to identify areas where the customer experience can be improved. By making the necessary changes, organizations are able to improve customer engagement and conversions.

Microsoft Dynamics CRM Customer Insights provides organizations with the ability to map and analyze customer journeys. This tool can help organizations to identify areas of improvement and to make the necessary changes to improve the customer experience. By using customer journey mapping and analysis, organizations are able to improve customer engagement and conversions.

6. Customer Lifetime Value and Churn Analysis in MS Dynamics CRM Customer Insights

Calculating customer lifetime value (CLV) and predicting churn in MS Dynamics CRM Customer Insights

CLV (customer lifetime value) is the metric that tells you how much revenue a customer will generate for your business over the course of their relationship with you. It's important to know your CLV because it helps you make decisions about how much to spend on acquisition and retention.

Churn is the percentage of customers who stop doing business with you over a given period of time. It's important to track churn because it can indicate problems with your product, your pricing, or your customer service.

MS Dynamics CRM Customer Insights is a tool that can help you with both CLV and churn analysis. With Customer Insights, you can segment your customers by CLV and then track churn rates for each segment. This information can help you make

decisions about where to focus your acquisition
and retention efforts.

Identifying high-value customers and implementing retention strategies in MS Dynamics CRM Customer Insights

As the Head of Customer Retention for a large e-
commerce company, I am always looking for ways
to identify our high-value customers and
implement strategies to keep them engaged with
our brand. I was recently introduced to MS
Dynamics CRM Customer Insights and was
impressed with its ability to help with both
customer lifetime value and churn analysis.

After importing our customer data into MS
Dynamics CRM Customer Insights, I was able to
quickly identify our top 10% most valuable
customers based on their lifetime value. I then
created a retention strategy tailored specifically to
this group of high-value customers.

The retention strategy included targeted
communications, exclusive offers, and a dedicated
customer service team. This dedicated team was
responsible for ensuring that our high-value

customers had a positive experience with our brand at every touchpoint.

Since implementing this retention strategy, we have seen a significant decrease in customer churn and an increase in customer lifetime value. I am confident that MS Dynamics CRM Customer Insights has been a key factor in our success.

Leveraging predictive analytics for CLV and churn analysis in MS Dynamics CRM Customer Insights

Leveraging predictive analytics for CLV and churn analysis in MS Dynamics CRM Customer Insights can help organizations better understand their customers and make more informed decisions about how to best grow their business. By understanding which customers are most likely to churn and why, organizations can take steps to improve customer retention and loyalty. Additionally, by understanding the lifetime value of their customers, organizations can make more informed decisions about marketing and sales strategies.

7. Marketing Campaign Analysis and Optimization in MS Dynamics CRM Customer Insights

Analyzing marketing campaign performance and attribution in MS Dynamics CRM Customer Insights

As the marketing director for a large company, you are always looking for ways to optimize your marketing campaigns and get the most return on investment (ROI). You have heard about MS Dynamics CRM Customer Insights and its ability to help with marketing campaign performance and attribution. After doing some research, you decide to give it a try.

You start by setting up a few test campaigns in MS Dynamics CRM Customer Insights. You are able to track each campaign's performance and see which channels are providing the most leads. You are also able to see which campaigns are resulting in the most sales.

After a few weeks of using MS Dynamics CRM Customer Insights, you are impressed with the results. You are able to see which campaigns are performing the best and make adjustments accordingly. You are also able to see which channels are providing the most leads and sales. Overall, you are able to get a better understanding of your marketing campaigns and how to optimize them for the best results.

A/B testing and optimization of marketing campaigns in MS Dynamics CRM Customer Insights

A/B testing is a method of marketing campaign optimization in which two or more versions of a campaign are tested against each other to determine which performs better. The goal of A/B testing is to improve the performance of a campaign by making it more effective at achieving its objectives.

MS Dynamics CRM Customer Insights is a powerful tool that can be used to analyze and optimize marketing campaigns. It provides a wealth of data that can be used to understand how a campaign is performing and to identify areas where it can be improved.

Customer Insights can be used to conduct A/B tests on marketing campaigns. This involves creating two or more versions of a campaign and testing them against each other. The results of the tests can be used to determine which version of the campaign is more effective at achieving its objectives.

A/B testing is an important tool that should be used to optimize marketing campaigns. It can help to improve the performance of a campaign and to make it more effective at achieving its objectives.

Utilizing customer insights for personalized and targeted marketing in MS Dynamics CRM Customer Insights

As the marketing landscape continues to evolve, so too must the way we utilize customer insights to inform our marketing efforts. No longer can we rely on a one-size-fits-all approach; instead, we must personalize our marketing campaigns to better target our audience and meet their needs.

MS Dynamics CRM Customer Insights provides the tools we need to collect and analyze customer data, so that we can identify trends and optimize our marketing campaigns accordingly. By understanding our customers better, we can create more targeted and effective marketing campaigns that will ultimately lead to improved ROI.

Here are just a few ways we can use MS Dynamics CRM Customer Insights to improve our marketing campaigns:

1. Segmentation: We can use customer insights to segment our audience into smaller, more manageable groups. This way, we can create more targeted marketing campaigns that are better suited to each group's needs.

2. Persona Development: By understanding our customer's wants, needs, and motivations, we can develop marketing personas. This helps us create more relatable and effective marketing campaigns.

3. Campaign Analysis and Optimization: We can use customer insights to analyze our past marketing campaigns and identify areas for improvement. This way, we can ensure that our future campaigns are more successful.

MS Dynamics CRM Customer Insights provides us with the valuable insights we need to create more personalized and targeted marketing campaigns. By understanding our customers better, we can improve our ROI and better meet their needs.

8. Sales Forecasting and Opportunity Analysis in MS Dynamics CRM Customer Insights

Forecasting sales revenue and pipeline using customer insights in MS Dynamics CRM Customer Insights

As the Sales Manager for my company, I am always looking for ways to improve our sales forecasting and pipeline analysis. I was recently introduced to MS Dynamics CRM Customer Insights and was intrigued by the potential it had for helping us gain a deeper understanding of our customers and their buying behavior. After doing some research, I decided to implement MS Dynamics CRM Customer Insights into our sales process.

So far, I have been very impressed with the results. MS Dynamics CRM Customer Insights has allowed us to get a much better understanding of our customers and their needs. This has in turn allowed us to more accurately forecast sales revenue and pipeline opportunities. Additionally, the platform has also been very helpful in identifying potential upsell and cross-sell opportunities. Overall, I am very pleased with the results we have seen so far and would recommend MS Dynamics CRM Customer Insights to any company looking to improve their sales forecasting and pipeline analysis.

Analyzing sales opportunities and identifying upsell and cross-sell opportunities in MS Dynamics CRM Customer Insights

As a sales representative, one of the most important aspects of my job is analyzing sales opportunities and identifying upsell and cross-sell opportunities. This allows me to forecast future sales and opportunities, and plan my sales strategy accordingly.

I use MS Dynamics CRM Customer Insights to help me with this task. The software provides me with valuable insights into customer behavior and trends. This information is essential in helping me identify which products or services my customers are most likely to be interested in.

By analyzing sales opportunities and identifying upsell and cross-sell opportunities, I am able to increase my sales and better serve my customers.

MS Dynamics CRM Customer Insights is a valuable tool that I would recommend to any sales representative.

Integrating customer insights with sales processes and workflows in MS Dynamics CRM Customer Insights

As the Head of Sales for a small-to-medium sized business, I am always looking for ways to optimize our sales processes and workflows. One way I recently discovered was integrating customer insights with our sales processes and workflows in MS Dynamics CRM Customer Insights. This has helped us immensely with sales forecasting and opportunity analysis.

Before, we would base our sales forecasts and opportunities off of historical data and gut instinct. However, this would often lead to inaccurate forecasts and missed opportunities. But by integrating customer insights into our sales processes, we are now able to get a much clearer picture of what our customers want and need. This has helped us to better forecast sales and opportunities, and has resulted in increased sales and profitability.

If you are looking for ways to improve your sales processes and workflows, I highly recommend integrating customer insights with your sales processes in MS Dynamics CRM Customer Insights. It has made a world of difference for us and I am confident it can do the same for you.

9. Customer Service and Support Analytics in MS Dynamics CRM Customer Insights

Analyzing customer service interactions and satisfaction metrics in MS Dynamics CRM Customer Insights

As the Manager of Customer Service and Support Analytics, I am responsible for analyzing customer service interactions and satisfaction metrics in MS Dynamics CRM Customer Insights. In this role, I work closely with the customer service team to identify areas of improvement and make recommendations for changes to the customer service process. I also use MS Dynamics CRM Customer Insights to track customer satisfaction levels and identify trends. By analyzing customer service interactions and satisfaction metrics, I am able to help the customer service team provide a better experience for our customers.

Implementing proactive support and personalized service strategies in MS Dynamics CRM Customer Insights

As the customer service and support manager for a large company, I was tasked with finding a way to improve our customer service and support analytics in MS Dynamics CRM Customer Insights. After doing some research, I decided that the best way to improve our customer service and support analytics was to implement proactive support and personalized service strategies.

Proactive support means that we would reach out to our customers before they had a chance to contact us. This would allow us to address any issues they were having before they even had a chance to become frustrated with our product or service.

Personalized service means that we would tailor our service to each individual customer. This would allow us to better meet their needs and expectations.

I implemented these two strategies by training our customer service and support staff on how to use MS Dynamics CRM Customer Insights. I also created templates and scripts that they could use to proactively reach out to customers and provide them with personalized service.

Since implementing these strategies, we have seen a significant improvement in our customer service and support analytics. Our customers are now more satisfied with our product and service, and we have seen a decrease in the number of customer service and support issues.

Utilizing sentiment analysis and customer feedback for service improvements in MS Dynamics CRM Customer Insights

Sentiment analysis and customer feedback are important tools that can be used to improve customer service and support analytics in MS Dynamics CRM Customer Insights. By analyzing customer sentiment, companies can identify areas where customers are unhappy and make changes to improve the customer experience. Additionally, customer feedback can be used to identify specific issues that need to be addressed and to track the progress of service improvements. By utilizing sentiment analysis and customer feedback, companies can make significant improvements to their customer service and support analytics.

10. Privacy and Data Governance in MS Dynamics CRM Customer Insights

Understanding data privacy regulations and compliance (e.g., GDPR, CCPA) in MS Dynamics CRM Customer Insights

As the use of MS Dynamics CRM Customer Insights continues to grow, so does the need to ensure that data privacy regulations and compliance requirements are met. The General Data Protection Regulation (GDPR) and the California Consumer Privacy Act (CCPA) are two of the most important data privacy regulations that companies must comply with.

GDPR requires companies to take steps to protect the personal data of EU citizens. This includes ensuring that personal data is collected and processed lawfully, transparently, and with the individual's consent. Companies must also take steps to ensure that personal data is accurate and up-to-date, and that individuals have the right to access their personal data and to have it erased if they no longer want it to be processed.

CCPA, on the other hand, requires companies to take steps to protect the personal data of California residents. This includes ensuring that personal data is collected and processed lawfully, transparently, and with the individual's consent. Companies must also take steps to ensure that personal data is accurate and up-to-date, and that individuals have the right to access their personal data and to opt out of its sale.

To ensure compliance with both GDPR and CCPA, MS Dynamics CRM Customer Insights has implemented a number of features and controls. For example, personal data is only collected and processed with the individual's consent, and individuals have the right to access their personal data and to have it erased. In addition, personal data is accuracy and up-to-date, and individuals have the right to opt out of its sale.

MS Dynamics CRM Customer Insights is committed to ensuring compliance with all data privacy regulations and requirements. We encourage our customers to review our privacy policy and terms of use to ensure that they understand how their personal data will be used and protected.

Implementing data governance and security measures in MS Dynamics CRM Customer Insights

As your organization looks to adopt or expand its use of Microsoft Dynamics CRM Customer Insights, it's important to consider privacy and data governance best practices. By taking a proactive approach to data governance and security, you can help ensure that your customer data is protected and your organization remains compliant with privacy regulations.

Here are some key considerations for privacy and data governance in Microsoft Dynamics CRM Customer Insights:

1. Establish a governance framework

Before you can start implementing privacy and data security measures, you need to establish a governance framework. This will help you define roles and responsibilities, set policies and procedures, and establish controls to ensure compliance.

2. Classify your data

One of the first steps in implementing a privacy and data governance program is to classify your data. This will help you determine which data is sensitive and needs to be protected.

3. Implement security controls

Once you've classified your data, you can start implementing security controls to protect it. This may include encryption, access controls, and activity monitoring.

4. Train your employees

It's important to train your employees on your privacy and data security policies and procedures. They should know how to handle sensitive data and what to do if they suspect a security breach.

5. Monitor and audit your data

Finally, you need to monitor and audit your data to ensure that your security controls are effective and that your employees are following your policies and procedures.

Ensuring ethical use of customer data and transparency in insights generation in MS Dynamics CRM Customer Insights

As the world increasingly moves online, companies are collecting more data than ever before on their customers. With this data comes a responsibility to ensure that it is used ethically and transparently.

Microsoft Dynamics CRM Customer Insights is a powerful tool that can help companies to better understand their customers and make better decisions about how to engage with them. However, it is important to ensure that this tool is used in a way that respects customer privacy and data governance.

When using MS Dynamics CRM Customer Insights, companies should be clear about what data they are collecting and why. They should also put in place measures to ensure that this data is used responsibly and only for legitimate business purposes.

Transparency is also important when using MS Dynamics CRM Customer Insights. Companies should be clear about how they are using the tool and what insights they are generating from it. They should also be open to feedback from customers about how they would like to see their data used.

By ensuring ethical use of customer data and transparency in insights generation, companies can build trust with their customers and show that they are committed to protecting their privacy.

11. Integration and Extensibility of MS Dynamics CRM Customer Insights

Integrating MS Dynamics CRM Customer Insights with other systems (e.g., CRM, marketing automation)

Organizations that use Microsoft Dynamics CRM Customer Insights can take advantage of its integration and extensibility capabilities to create a more seamless and personalized customer experience. By integrating MS Dynamics CRM Customer Insights with other systems, organizations can create a single view of the customer across all touchpoints and channels. Additionally, integration and extensibility can enable organizations to automate customer journeys, create personalized marketing campaigns, and measure the impact of customer engagement.

Extending the functionality of MS Dynamics CRM Customer Insights through customizations, plugins, and workflows

As your business grows, so does your customer base. To keep up with the demand, you need a customer relationship management (CRM) system that can scale with you. Microsoft Dynamics CRM Customer Insights is a powerful CRM system that can be customized and extended to meet the needs of your business.

Through customizations, plugins, and workflows, you can extend the functionality of MS Dynamics CRM Customer Insights to better meet the needs of your business. For example, you can integrate MS Dynamics CRM Customer Insights with your accounting software to keep track of invoices and payments. You can also extend the system to include features such as loyalty programs and customer portals.

Workflows can automate tasks such as sending thank-you emails to customers after a purchase. By customizing and extending MS Dynamics CRM Customer Insights, you can make the system work exactly the way you need it to.

Integration of MS Dynamics CRM Customer Insights with external analytics and business intelligence tools

As the demand for customer insights grows, so does the need for integration with external analytics and business intelligence tools. By integrating MS Dynamics CRM Customer Insights with these tools, organizations can gain a more complete picture of their customers and make better decisions about how to engage with them.

External analytics and business intelligence tools can provide a wealth of data that can be used to improve customer insights. By integrating these tools with Customer Insights, organizations can gain access to more data points and get a more complete picture of their customers. This data can be used to segment customers, understand their needs and wants, and develop targeted marketing and sales strategies.

Integrating MS Dynamics CRM Customer Insights with external analytics and business intelligence tools can help organizations to better understand their customers and make more informed decisions about how to engage with them. This integration can help organizations to improve

customer satisfaction and loyalty, and to increase
sales and revenue.

12. Best Practices and Advanced Tips for MS Dynamics CRM Customer Insights

Implementing industry best practices for customer insights management

The goal of customer insights management is to ensure that an organization is able to make the most of its customer data. To do this, it is important to implement industry best practices. Here are some tips for doing so:

1. Establish a clear goal for customer insights management. What does your organization hope to achieve by leveraging customer data? This could be anything from improving customer retention to increasing sales.

2. Create a customer data governance policy. This policy should outline how customer data will be collected, stored, and used. It should also identify who is responsible for managing customer data.

3. Make sure customer data is of high quality. This means ensuring that data is accurate and complete. It also means ensuring that data is timely, so that it can be used to make decisions about current and future customer interactions.

4. Use customer data to create actionable insights. Insights should be used to inform decisions about marketing, sales, and customer service. They should also be used to improve the customer experience.

5. Continuously monitor and improve customer insights management. This includes regularly reviewing data quality and customer data governance policies. It also includes constantly looking for new ways to use customer data to improve the business.

Handling complex data scenarios and challenges in MS Dynamics CRM Customer Insights

As your organization's data grows and becomes more complex, Microsoft Dynamics CRM Customer Insights can help you make sense of it all and glean valuable insights. Here are some best practices and advanced tips to get the most out of this powerful tool:

1. When working with large data sets, it's important to first filter down to the specific records you want to analyze. This will help

improve performance and avoid overwhelming the system.

2. Use the "Preview with Sampled Data" feature to test out your analysis on a smaller subset of data before running it on the entire dataset. This can help you catch any errors or issues before they cause problems.

3. Take advantage of the "What-If Analysis" feature to test out different scenarios and see how they would impact your results. This is a great way to explore different options and find the best solution for your needs.

4. Use the "Export Data" feature to download your results for further analysis or for use in other reporting tools. This is a great way to share your findings with others or to keep a backup of your data.

5. Keep in mind that Microsoft Dynamics CRM Customer Insights is constantly evolving and adding new features. Be sure to stay up-to-date on the latest changes so you can take advantage of everything it has to offer.

Optimizing performance and scalability of the Customer Insights Module

As your business grows, so does your customer base. And with more customers comes more data. The Customer Insights Module in Microsoft Dynamics CRM is designed to help you make sense of all this data, and optimize your performance and scalability. Here are some best practices and advanced tips to help you get the most out of the Customer Insights Module:

1. Use the Data Explorer to segment your data.

The Data Explorer is a powerful tool that lets you segment your data in a variety of ways. This is useful for understanding your customer base and finding trends.

2. Use Advanced Find to create custom reports.

Advanced Find is a great way to create custom reports. You can use it to find specific data, or to create reports that show trends over time.

3. Use the Data Viewer to visualize your data.

The Data Viewer is a helpful tool that lets you visualize your data in a variety of ways. This can be useful for understanding your data, or for finding trends.

4. Use the Query Builder to create custom reports.

The Query Builder is a powerful tool that lets you create custom reports. You can use it to find specific data, or to create reports that show trends over time.

5. Use the Report Wizard to create custom reports.

The Report Wizard is a helpful tool that lets you create custom reports. You can use it to find specific data, or to create reports that show trends over time.

6. Use the Scheduler to automate report generation.

The Scheduler is a helpful tool that lets you automate report generation. This can be useful for ensuring that you always have the latest data, or for reducing the workload on your team.

7. Use the Report Viewer to view reports.

The Report Viewer is a helpful tool that lets you view reports. This can be useful for understanding your data, or for finding trends.

8. Use the Dashboard to visualize your data.

The Dashboard is a helpful tool that lets you visualize your data. This can be useful for understanding your data, or for finding trends.

9. Use the Map Viewer to visualize your data.

The Map Viewer is a helpful tool that lets you visualize your data. This can be useful for understanding your data, or for finding trends.

10. Use the Export Wizard to export your data.

The Export Wizard is a helpful tool that lets you export your data. This can be useful for sharing data with other teams, or for creating backups.

13. Future Trends and Developments in MS Dynamics CRM Customer Insights

Exploring the latest features and updates in MS Dynamics CRM Customer Insights Module

The Microsoft Dynamics CRM Customer Insights Module is constantly evolving to meet the needs of today's businesses. The latest features and updates make it even easier to use and more powerful than ever. Here's a look at some of the latest trends and developments in the MS Dynamics CRM Customer Insights Module.

One of the latest trends is the use of artificial intelligence (AI) to help businesses better understand their customers. AI can be used to analyze customer data and identify patterns and trends. This information can then be used to create targeted marketing campaigns and improve customer service.

Another trend is the use of social media data to improve customer insights. Social media data can be used to track customer sentiment and identify issues that are important to them. This information can then be used to create targeted marketing campaigns and improve customer service.

The latest updates to the MS Dynamics CRM Customer Insights Module make it even easier to use and more powerful than ever. The new features and updates include:

- An improved user interface that makes it easier to navigate and use the module

- Improved data visualization that makes it easier to see patterns and trends

- Improved reporting that makes it easier to track progress and results

- A new customer segmentation tool that makes it easier to target marketing campaigns

- A new customer profile tool that makes it easier to understand customer needs

- A new customer journey tool that makes it easier to track and improve the customer experience

The MS Dynamics CRM Customer Insights Module is a powerful tool that can help businesses improve their customer relationships. The latest trends and developments make it even more powerful and easy to use.

Understanding the roadmap and future direction of the Customer Insights Module

The Microsoft Dynamics CRM Customer Insights Module is a powerful tool that helps organizations to understand their customers and make better decisions about how to engage with them. The module provides a 360-degree view of the customer, including their demographics, preferences, and behavior. It also includes a predictive analytics engine that can help organizations to identify trends and make predictions about future customer behavior.

The Customer Insights Module is constantly evolving, and Microsoft is always adding new features and functionality to the module. In the future, we expect the module to become even more powerful and user-friendly. Microsoft is also working on integrating the Customer Insights Module with other Microsoft products, such as Power BI and Excel, to make it even easier for organizations to use the module and get the most out of it.

Overall, the Microsoft Dynamics CRM Customer Insights Module is a valuable tool that will continue to help organizations to better understand their customers and make more informed decisions about how to engage with them.

Predicting and discussing emerging trends in customer data analytics and insights

The future of customer data analytics and insights is looking very promising. With the advent of new technologies, there is a lot of potential for businesses to gain a deeper understanding of their customers and their needs. Here are some emerging trends that are worth keeping an eye on:

1. Increased use of artificial intelligence (AI) and machine learning (ML)

AI and ML are already being used by some businesses to help them analyze customer data more effectively. However, these technologies are still in their infancy and there is a lot of potential for them to be used even more extensively in the future. Businesses that are able to harness the power of AI and ML will be able to gain a competitive edge by being able to better understand their customers and provide them with the products and services they need.

2. Greater use of customer data

As businesses become more data-driven, they will increasingly rely on customer data to help them make decisions. This data can come from a variety of sources, including social media, surveys, customer feedback, and transactional data. By analyzing this data, businesses will be able to gain insights into what their customers want and need, and they will be able to tailor their offerings accordingly.

3. More personalized experiences

As businesses become better at understanding their customers, they will also be able to provide them with more personalized experiences. This could include things like personalized product recommendations, targeted marketing messages, and customized customer service. By providing customers with experiences that are tailored to their individual needs, businesses will be able to build deeper relationships with them and increase loyalty.

4. Increased focus on customer retention

With the increase in competition, businesses will need to focus more on retaining their existing customers. This will require a shift in focus from acquisition to retention. Businesses will need to find ways to keep their customers happy and engaged, and they will need to provide them with the support they need to stay with the company.

5. Greater use of customer data to improve business operations

Customer data can be used for more than just marketing and customer service. It can also be used to improve a variety of business operations, including product development, supply chain management, and financial planning. By using customer data to improve their operations, businesses will be able to boost their efficiency and bottom line.

These are just a few of the emerging trends in customer data analytics and insights. As businesses become more data-driven, they will need to pay close attention to these trends in order to stay ahead of the competition.

www.ingramcontent.com/pod-product-compliance
Lightning Source LLC
LaVergne TN
LVHW051614050326
832903LV00033B/4504